The
Tao
te
Ching
of
Lao
Tzu

Also by Brian Browne Walker

The I Ching or Book of Changes:
  A Guide to Life's Turning Points

Hua Hu Ching: The Unknown Teachings of Lao Tzu

The Crazy Dog Guide to Lifetime Happiness

The Crazy Dog Guide to Happier Work

the Tao te Ching of Lao Tzu

St.
Martin's
Griffin
New
York

A New
Translation by

**Brian
Browne
Walker**

Design by Jaye Zimet

Library of Congress Cataloging-in-Publication Data

Lao tzu.
  [The Tao te ching. English]
The Tao te ching / translation by Brian Browne Walker.
      p. cm.
    ISBN 0-312-14744-9
    I. Walker, Brian Browne.   II. Title.
BL1900.L26E5   1995
299'.51482—dc20   95-4457
                        CIP

10 9 8 7 6

this book is
"livicated" to
the memories of
Colin and
Max,
TO
the immortal
illuminating
presence of the
Hon. Robert
Nesta Marley,
O.M.,
TO
my teacher,
smiling
Qalandari uncle,
and gracious friend,
Elias Velonis
Amidon
TO
Rabbia, gentle,
generous,
loving friend and,
as always,
TO
my darling
daughter, my little
dancer, me lickle
Rasta girl,
Sofia Sofia
Muhammad
Ali

I gratefully
acknowledge
the wind and rain,
the snow, the sun,
each and every one
of the trees, the water
singing under the
ice of frozen
rivers, the
mountains
and valleys, the
cold ground and the
warm grass, the
light and the
darkness, the
creatures,
poetry, music,
family, friends,
the gift and
mystery of my
life, the eternal
Tao.

The *Tao te Ching* of Lao Tzu is one of the most frequently translated, widely read, and deeply cherished books in the world. It is, to my mind, the wisest book ever written and one of the greatest gifts ever given to humankind. In the handful of pages that make up the *Tao te Ching*, I believe there is an answer to each of life's questions, a solution to every predicament, a balm for any wound. It is less a book than a living, breathing angel.

How wonderfully ironic that a book as profound and simple as this bears a title that is difficult to translate. The word *tao* has no close equivalent in our language. "The Way" is one translation; "the way the universe works" is another; neither is wholly satisfactory. It is fitting that the word remains enigmatic, because the idea behind it is *the* essential enigma: We know that life and the universe have a source, but the nature and depth of that source lie beyond our ken.

As for the rest of the title, *te* may be translated as "goodness," "virtue," or "nature"; *ching* means "book" or "sutra" or "scripture." What do we end up with? "The Book of the Good and Natural Way"?

Lao Tzu is no less an enigma. His name is generally translated as "old sage," or, less often, "old boy." My personal translation would be something like "ancient infant," which suggests the combination of wisdom and suppleness that his philosophy embodies.

According to legend, Lao Tzu was keeper of the Imperial Archives, in what is now China, during the Chou Dynasty some twenty-six hundred years ago. During a period of chaos and disorder, he elected to leave civiliza tion and go to live out his life alone in the mountains. As he approached the gate of the city, riding on the back of an ox, he was stopped by the gatekeeper. Learning of Lao Tzu's intentions, the man begged him to leave some written expression of his wisdom for the benefit of others. And so, the story goes, the *Tao te Ching* came into being.

Another delightful Lao Tzu story is in wide circu- lation. As Witter Bynner tells it in his book *The Way of Life According to Lao Tzu* (Capricorn Books, 1944):

> Confucius, impressed by Lao Tzu's influence
> on people, visited him once to ask advice,
> ironically enough, on points of ceremonial
> etiquette. Baffled by the answers of the older
> man, to whom etiquette meant hypocrisy and
> nonsense, Confucius returned to his disciples
> and told them, "Of birds I know that they have
> wings to fly with, of fish that they have fins to
> swim with, of wild beasts that they have feet to
> run with. For feet there are traps, for fins nets,
> for wings arrows. But who knows how dragons
> surmount wind and cloud into heaven? This
> day I have seen Lao Tzu and he is a dragon.

That Lao Tzu was a dragon is certain. Whether he was ever an actual lone man is doubtful. Historical evidence suggests otherwise. What is more likely is that the body of teachings now known as the *Tao te Ching* was developed over a period of two or three hundred years by five or six different sages. Some were almost assuredly women; certainly the teaching here is the gentlest and most motherly of all the world's great books on the art of living.

In the end it matters little who or what Lao Tzu was. As I wrote in my translation of the *Hua Hu Ching*, "I have come to think of Lao Tzu less as a man who once lived and more as a song that plays, eternal and abiding." As with any great song, there are many great versions. I highly recommend to students of Tao that they study various translations of the *Tao te Ching*. I have endeavored in my own to stay as close as possible to the direct literal translation of the Chinese characters; in a very few places, it proved impossible to do that and get the proper idea across, and in those instances I have used the minimal amount of poetic license necessary to effectively communicate the teaching.

There are other translations that also achieve a high degree of literal accuracy. Of the ones I know, I often recommend the one written by Ellen M. Chen. Her commentary on the text is illuminating. Among the translations that take more significant liberties with the text in the interest of poetry, my personal favorites are those of Stephen Mitchell and Witter Bynner. For all the offense Bynner gives academic Taoists (he neither read nor spoke Chinese), his book is as lively, lovely, and unruly as it was when it was published over fifty years ago. Though he did not understand Chinese, he clearly heard and understood Lao Tzu. May we all be as fortunate.

—Brian Browne Walker
Boulder, Colorado

There is no question of time and space. Understanding depends on ripeness of mind. What does it matter if one lives in the East or in the West?

—Ramana Maharshi

The

Tao

te

Ching

of

Lao

Tzu

1

Tao is beyond words
        and beyond understanding.
Words may be used to speak of it,
        but they cannot contain it.

Tao existed before words and names,
        before heaven and earth,
        before the ten thousand things.
It is the unlimited father and mother
        of all limited things.

Therefore, to see beyond boundaries
        to the subtle heart of things,
        dispense with names,
        with concepts,
        with expectations and ambitions and differences.

Tao and its many manifestations
        arise from the same source:
        subtle wonder within mysterious darkness.

This is the beginning of all understanding.

2

When people find one thing beautiful,
　　another consequently becomes ugly.
When one man is held up as good,
　　another is judged deficient.

Similarly, being and nonbeing balance each other;
　　difficult and easy define each other;
　　long and short illustrate each other;
　　high and low rest upon one another;
　　voice and song meld into harmony;
　　what is to come follows upon what has been.

The wise person acts without effort
　　and teaches by quiet example.
He accepts things as they come,
　　creates without possessing,
　　nourishes without demanding,
　　accomplishes without taking credit.

Because he constantly forgets himself,
　　he is never forgotten.

3

When praise is lavished upon the famous,
  the people contend and compete with one another.
When exotic goods are traded and treasured,
  the compulsion to steal is felt.
When desires are constantly stimulated,
  people become disturbed and confused.

Therefore, the wise person sets an example by
  emptying her mind,
  opening her heart,
  relaxing her ambitions,
  relinquishing her desires,
  cultivating her character.
Having conquered her own cunning and cravings,
  she can't be manipulated by anyone.

Do by not-doing.
Act with nonaction.
Allow order to arise of itself.

4

Tao is a whirling emptiness,
    yet when used it cannot be exhausted.
Out of this mysterious well
    flows everything in existence.

Blunting sharp edges,
Untangling knots,
Softening the glare,
Settling the dust,
It evolves us all and
    makes the whole world one.

Something is there, hidden in the deep!
But I do not know whose child it is—
It came even before God.

5

Heaven and earth are not sentimental;
    they regard all things as dispensable.
The sage isn't sentimental, either;
    He views all forms as ephemeral and transitional.

Tao is like a bellows:
    empty, but inexhaustible.
The more you move it, the more it makes.
Too much talk about it evaporates your
    understanding, though.

Simply stay at the center of the circle.

6

The heart of Tao is immortal,
    the mysterious fertile mother of us all,
        of heaven and earth,
           of every thing
             and not-thing.

Invisible yet ever-present,
    you can use it forever without using it up.

Heaven is eternal, earth everlasting.
They endure this way because they
      do not live for themselves.

In the same way, the wise person
      puts himself last,
      and thereby finds himself first;

      Holds himself outside,
      and thereby remains at the center;

      Abandons himself,
      and is thereby fulfilled.

8

The highest good is like water
    which benefits all things
    and contends with none.
It flows in low places that others disdain
    and thus is close to the Tao.

In living, choose your ground well.
In thought, stay deep in the heart.
In relationship, be generous.
In speaking, hold to truth.
In leadership, be organized.
In work, do your best.
In action, be timely.

If you compete with no one,
    no one can compete with you.

Filling to fullness is not as good
    as stopping at the right moment.
Oversharpening a blade causes its edge
    to be lost.
Line your home with treasures and you
    won't be able to defend it.

Amass possessions,
    establish positions,
    display your pride:
Soon enough disaster drives you to your knees.

This is the way of heaven:
    do your work, then quietly step back.

10

Can you marry your spirit and body to
    the oneness and never depart from it?
Can you ride your breath until your entire
    being is as supple as the body of an infant?
Can you cleanse your inner vision until you
    see heaven in every direction?
Can you love people and govern them without
    conniving and manipulating?
Can you bear heaven's children in all that
    you do and are?
Can you give the wisdom of your heart precedence
    over the learning of your head?

Giving birth,
    nourishing life,
    shaping things without possessing them,
    serving without expectation of reward,
    leading without dominating:
These are the profound virtues of nature,
    and of nature's best beings.

11

Thirty spokes meet at a hollowed-out hub;
    the wheel won't work without its hole.
A vessel is moulded from solid clay;
    its inner emptiness makes it useful.
To make a room, you have to cut doors and windows;
    without openings, a place isn't livable.

To make use of what is here,
    you must make use of what is not.

12

The five colors blind the eye.
The five tones deafen the ear.
The five flavors overwhelm the palate.

Fancy things get in the way of one's growth.
Racing here and there,
      hunting for this and that—
Good ways to madden your mind, that's all.

Relinquish what is without.
Cultivate what is within.
Live for your center, not your senses.

Favor and disgrace are equally problematic.
Hope and fear are phantoms of the body.

What does it mean that "favor and disgrace
    are equally problematic"?
Favor lifts you up; disgrace knocks you down.
Either one depends on the opinions of others and
    causes you to depart from your center.

What does it mean that "hope and fear are
    phantoms of the body"?
When you regard your body as your self,
    hope and fear have real power over you.
If you abandon the notion of body as self,
    hope and fear cannot touch you.

Know the universe as your self, and
    you can live absolutely anywhere in comfort.
Love the world as your self, and
    you'll be able to care for it properly.

14

Looked at but not seen,
    listened to but not heard,
    grasped for but not held,
    formless, soundless, intangible:
the Tao resists analysis and
    defies comprehension.

Its rising is not about light,
    its setting not a matter of darkness.
Unnameable, unending,
    emerging continually, and
    continually pouring back into nothingness,
It is formless form, unseeable image,
    elusive evasive unimaginable mystery.

Confront it, and you won't see its face.
Follow it, and you can't find an end.
Perceive its ancient subtle heart, however,
    and you become master of the moment.
Know what came before time,
    and the beginning of wisdom is yours.

A sage is subtle, intuitive,
      penetrating, profound.
His depths are mysterious and unfathomable.
The best one can do is describe his appearance:

The sage is as alert as a person crossing
      a winter stream;
      as circumspect as a person with neighbors
          on all four sides;
      as respectful as a thoughtful guest;
      as yielding as melting ice;
      as simple as uncarved wood;
      as open as a valley;
      as chaotic as a muddy torrent.

Why "chaotic as a muddy torrent"?
Because clarity is learned by being
      patient in the presence of chaos.
Tolerating disarray, remaining at rest,
      gradually one learns to allow muddy water
          to settle and proper responses to
             reveal themselves.

Those who aspire to Tao don't long
    for fulfillment.
They selflessly allow the Tao to
    use and deplete them;
They calmly allow the Tao to
    renew and complete them.

Work toward emptiness and openness.
Cultivate stillness.
Breathe harmony.
Become tranquility.
As the ten thousand things rise and fall,
    rise and fall,
        just witness their return to the root.

Everything that flourishes dissolves
    again into the source.
To dissolve back into the source is to find peace.
To find peace is to recover your true nature.
To recover your nature is to know the
    constancy of Tao.
To know the constancy of Tao is insight.

Insight opens your mind.
An open mind leads to an open heart.
Openheartedness leads to justice.
Justice is an expression of divinity.
Divinity is oneness with Tao.
Oneness with Tao is freedom from harm,
    indescribable pleasure, eternal life.

17

The best leader is one whose existence
        is barely known.
Next best is one who is loved and praised.
Next is one who is feared.
Worst of all is a leader who is despised.

If you fail to trust people,
        they won't turn out to be trustworthy.

Therefore, guide others by quietly relying on Tao.
Then, when the work is done, the people can say,
"We did this ourselves."

18

When people lose sight of the Tao,
      codes of morality and justice are created.
When cleverness and strategies are in use,
      hypocrites are everywhere.

When families forego natural harmony,
      parents become pious and children
          become dutiful.
When the nation is reigned by darkness,
      patriotic advisers abound.

19

Give up religiosity and knowledge, and
      people will benefit a hundredfold.
Discard morality and righteousness, and
      people will return to natural love.
Abandon shrewdness and profiteering, and
      there won't be any robbers or thieves.

These are external matters, however.
What is most important is what happens within:
      look to what is pure;
      hold to what is simple;
      let go of self-interest;
      temper your desires.

Be done with knowing and your worries
        will disappear.
How much difference is there between yes and no?
How much distinction between good and evil?
Fearing what others fear, admiring
        what they admire—
                nonsense.

Conventional people are jolly and reckless,
        feasting on worldly things and carrying
                on as though every day were the
                        beginning of spring.
I alone remain uncommitted, like an
        infant who hasn't yet smiled:
                lost, quietly drifting, unattached
                        to ideas and places and things.

Conventional people hoard more than they need,
       but I possess nothing at all,
          know nothing at all,
             understanding nothing at all.
They are bright; I am dark.
They are sharp; I am dull.
Like the sea, I am calm and indifferent.
Like the wind, I have no particular direction.

Everyone else takes his place and does his job;
       I alone remain wild and natural and free.
I am different from others: my sustenance
      comes directly from the Mother.

21

The greatest virtue is to follow Tao,
    and only Tao.
You might say, "But Tao is illusive!
    Evasive! Mysterious! Dark!
      How can one follow that?"

By following this:
Out of silent subtle mystery emerge images.
These images coalesce into forms.
Within each form is contained the seed
    and essence of life.
Thus do all things emerge and expand out
    of darkness and emptiness.

Because its essence is real and evident
in the origins of all things,
the name of the Tao has survived
since the beginning of time.
How can I know the circumstances of the
origins of all things?
Exactly by this phenomenon.*

*With a deep bow to Whiskers Men-Ching and his translators.

Allow yourself to yield, and
    you can stay centered.
Allow yourself to bend, and
    you will stay straight.
Allow yourself to be empty, and
    you'll get filled up.
Allow yourself to be exhausted, and
    you'll be renewed.

Having little, you can receive much.
Having much, you'll just become confused.

Therefore the sage embraces the oneness
    and becomes a pattern for the whole world.
She doesn't display herself,
    so she becomes illuminated.
She doesn't justify herself,
    so she becomes distinguished.
She doesn't boast,
    so she is recognized.
She doesn't claim credit,
    so she advances and endures.
She doesn't contend,
    so no one can contend with her.

"Yield and you can stay centered"—
Is this saying meaningless?
Stay whole, and all things return to you.

Nature is sparing with speech:
    a whirlwind doesn't last all morning;
    a rain shower doesn't last all day.

What causes these? Heaven and earth.
If heaven and earth can't make something
    furious endure, how could man?

Concentrate on Tao and you'll experience Tao.
Concentrate on power and you'll experience power.
Concentrate on loss and you'll experience loss.

If you won't trust, you won't be trusted.

24

A man who tiptoes can't stand.
A man who straddles can't walk.
A man who shows off can't shine.

A man who justifies his actions isn't respected.
A man who boasts of his achievements has no merit.
A man who brags will not endure.

To a person of Tao, these things are
        excess food and superfluous behavior.
Because nothing good can come of them,
        he doesn't indulge in them.

25

Something mysterious and perfect existed
　　before even heaven and earth were born.
Silent, immeasurable,
　　standing alone and unchanging,
　　moving without end or exhaustion,
　　it is the mother of the known and unknown
　　　　universe.
I don't know its name, so I call it by
　　an alias: Tao.
Forced to describe it, I only say, "It is great."

That which is great continues.
That which continues goes far.
That which goes far returns.

Therefore Tao is great,
　　heaven is great,
　　earth is great,
　　a person of Tao is great.
These are the four greatnesses in the universe.

A person of Tao follows earth.
Earth follows heaven.
Heaven follows Tao.
Tao follows its own nature.

Heaviness is the root of lightness.
Tranquility is the master of agitation.

That is why the sage travels all day
    without ever losing sight of her baggage.
She may live in a glorious palace, but
    she isn't attached to its pleasures.

Why should the lord of ten thousand chariots
    behave lightly in the world?
One who acts lightly loses her foundation.
One who becomes agitated sacrifices her mastery.

27

A good runner leaves no tracks;
A good speaker makes no slips;
A good planner doesn't have to scheme.
The best lock has no bolt, and
      no one can open it.
The best knot uses no rope, and
      no one can untie it.

Thus the master is always good at saving
      people, and doesn't abandon anyone;
Always good at saving things, and
      doesn't waste anything.
This is known as "following the light."

What is a good man but a bad man's teacher?
What is a bad man but a good man's charge?
It doesn't matter how smart you are if you
      don't have the sense to honor your teachers
        and cherish your responsibilities.
This is an essential teaching of Tao.

To know the masculine and yet cleave to the
     feminine is to be the womb for the world.
Being the womb for the world, never departing
     from the eternal power of Tao,
          you become as an infant once again: immortal.

To know the bright and yet hold to the dull
     is to be the example for the world.
Being the example for the world, not deviating
     from the everlasting power of Tao,
          you return to the infinite once again:
               limitless.

To know honor and yet keep to humility
     is to be the valley for the world.
Being the valley for the world,
     rich with the primal power of Tao,
          you return once again to simplicity,
             like uncarved wood.

Allow Tao to carve you into a vessel for Tao.
Then you can serve the world without
     mutilating it.

29

If you try to grab hold of the world
      and do what you want with it,
          you won't succeed.
The world is a vessel for spirit, and
      it wasn't made to be manipulated.
Tamper with it, and you'll spoil it.
Hold it, and you'll lose it.

With Tao, sometimes you move ahead
      and sometimes you stay back;
Sometimes you work hard
      and sometimes you rest;
Sometimes you're strong
      and sometimes you're weak;
Sometimes you're up;
      sometimes you're down.

The sage remains sensitive,
      avoiding extremes,
      avoiding extravagance,
      avoiding excess.

30

Those who wish to use Tao to influence others
      don't rely on force or weapons or
         military strategies.
Force rebounds.
Weapons turn on their wielders.
Battles are inevitably followed by famines.

Just do what needs to be done, and then stop.
Attain your purpose, but don't press
      your advantage.
Be resolute, but don't boast.
Succeed, but don't crow.
Accomplish, but don't overpower.

Overdoing things invites decay,
      and this is against Tao.
Whatever is against Tao soon ceases to be.

31

Weapons are tools of evil, shunned and
    avoided by everything in nature.
Because people of Tao follow nature,
    they want nothing to do with weapons.

Unevolved people are eager to act out of strength,
    but a person of Tao values peace and quiet.
He knows that every being is born of the
    womb of Tao.
This means that his enemies are his enemies
    second, his own brothers and sisters first.

Thus he resorts to weapons only in the direst
    necessity, and then uses them with
        utmost restraint.
He takes no pleasure in victory, because
    to rejoice in victory is to delight in killing.
Whoever delights in killing will not find
    success in this world.

Observe victories as you observe a
    death in the family: with sorrow and mourning.
Every victory is a funeral for kin.

The primal eternal Tao is an unnameable
    simplicity.
Though small, there is nothing under all of
    heaven that can subjugate it.

If a leader abides by it, all beings are
    naturally drawn to him.
Heaven and earth come together in harmony
    and sweet rain falls everywhere.
People cooperate voluntarily, without
    any instruction.

When this simplicity is divided, every thing
    and not-thing needs a name.
Once there are names, the process of
    distinction should stop.
To know when to stop is to be free from danger.

Tao in the world is like streams flowing
    into the sea.

33

Knowing others is intelligence;
    knowing the self is enlightenment.
Conquering others is power;
    conquering the self is strength.

Know what is enough, and you'll be rich.
Persevere, and you'll develop a will.
Remain in the center, and you'll always
    be at home.
Die without dying, and you'll endure forever.

The great Tao floods and flows in
    every direction.
Everything in existence depends on it,
    and it doesn't deny them.
It accomplishes its work without naming or
    making claims for itself.

Everything in existence is clothed and
    nourished by it, but it doesn't lord
        over anything.
Aimless, ambitionless, it might be called "small."

Everything in existence returns to it, and
    still it doesn't lord over anything.
Thus it might also be called "great."

Because it has no desire to be great,
    it can achieve greatness.

35

Stay centered in the Tao and the world
    comes to you:
Comes, and isn't harmed;
Comes, and finds contentment.

Most travelers are drawn to music and good food.
When Tao is talked about, the words can seem
    bland and flavorless.

Looked at, it may not catch the eye.
Listened to, it might not seduce the ear.
Used, it can never be exhausted.

36

What is ultimately to be reduced
      must first be expanded.
What is ultimately to be weakened
      must first be made strong.
What is ultimately to be discarded
      must first be embraced.
What is ultimately to be taken away
      must first be given.
This is called subtle insight.

The soft overcomes the hard.
The weak overcomes the strong.
The Tao should never be abandoned.
Weapons should never be displayed.

37

Eternal Tao doesn't do anything,
      yet it leaves nothing undone.
If you abide by it, everything
      in existence will transform itself.

When, in the process of self-transformation,
      desires are aroused, calm them with
            nameless simplicity.
When desires are dissolved in the primal presence,
      peace and harmony naturally occur,
            and the world orders itself.

38

A truly good person doesn't dwell on her goodness.
Thus she can be truly good.
A person of false goodness never forgets her
goodness.
Thus her goodness is always false.

A truly good person does nothing,
yet nothing remains undone.
A person of false goodness is forever doing,
yet everything remains forever undone.

Those who are interested in service act
without motive.
Those who are interested in righteousness
act with motives of all sorts.
Those who are interested in propriety act,
and receiving no response, they roll up
their sleeves and use force.

When Tao is lost, goodness appears.
When goodness is lost, philanthropy appears.
When philanthropy is lost, justice appears.
When justice is lost, only etiquette is left.

Etiquette is the faintest husk of real loyalty
     and faith, and it is the beginning of confusion.
Knowledge of the future is only a blossom of Tao;
     to become preoccupied with it is folly.

Thus the sage sets her sights on the substance
     and not the surface, on the fruit and
          not the flower.
Leaving the one, she gains the other.

39

From ancient times these have attained
    oneness with Tao:
Heaven attained oneness and became clear.
Earth attained oneness and became peaceful.
Spirits attained oneness and became strong.
Valleys attained oneness and became full.
Beings attained oneness and became fertile.
Sages attained oneness and became whole.
All are what they are by virtue of oneness.

Heaven without clarity would fall.
Earth without peace would explode.
Spirits without strength would dissipate.
Valleys without fullness would dry up.
Beings without fertility would die off.
Sages without wholeness would stumble and fall.

Humility is the root of greatness.
Those in high positions do well to think of
      themselves as powerless, small, and unworthy.
Isn't this taking humility for the root?

Attain honor without being honored.
Don't shine like jade, or chime like bells.

Returning to the root is the movement of Tao.
Quietness is how it functions.

The ten thousand things are born of being.
Being is born of nonbeing.

41

When a wise person hears Tao,
    he practices it diligently.
When an average person hears Tao,
    he practices it sometimes,
        and just as often ignores it.
When an inferior person hears Tao,
    he roars with laughter.
If he didn't laugh, it wouldn't be Tao.

Thus the age-old sayings:
The way to illumination appears dark.
The way that advances appears to retreat.
The way that is easy appears to be hard.
The highest virtue appears empty.
The purest goodness appears soiled.
The most profound creativity appears fallow.
The strongest power appears weak.
The most genuine appears unreal.
The greatest space has no corners.
The greatest talent matures slowly.
The greatest voice can't be heard.
The greatest image can't be seen.

Tao is hidden and has no name.
Tao alone nourishes and fulfills all things.

42

Nonbeing gives birth to the oneness.
The oneness gives birth to yin and yang.
Yin and yang give birth to heaven, earth,
    and beings.
Heaven, earth, and beings give birth to
    everything in existence.

Therefore everything in existence carries
    within it both yin and yang, and attains
    its harmony by blending together
    these two vital breaths.

Ordinary people hate nothing more than to be
    powerless, small, and unworthy.
Yet this is how superior people
    describe themselves.
Gain is loss.
Loss is gain.

I repeat what others have said:
The strong and violent don't die natural deaths.
This is the very essence of my teaching.

43

The soft overcomes the hard in the world
     as a gentle rider controls a galloping horse.

That without substance can penetrate where
     there is no space.

By these I know the benefit of nonaction.
Teaching without words, working without actions—
     nothing in the world can compare with them.

44

Which is more precious, fame or health?
Which is more valuable, health or wealth?
Which is more harmful, winning or losing?

The more excessive your love,
    the greater your suffering.
The larger your hoard,
    the heavier your losses.

Knowing what is enough is freedom.
Knowing when to stop is safety.
Practice these, and you'll endure.

The greatest perfection seems imperfect,
    yet its usefulness is endless.
The greatest fullness seems empty,
    yet its usefulness is inexhaustible.

Great straightness seems flexible.
Great skill looks clumsy.
Great eloquence sounds awkward.

Movement triumphs over cold.
Stillness triumphs over heat.
Clarity and tranquility set the
    whole world in order.

46

When the world practices Tao,
    horses fertilize the fields.
When the world ignores Tao,
    horses are bred for war.

There is no greater calamity than desire,
    no greater curse than greed.
Know that enough is enough,
    and you'll always have enough.

Without going out the door,
    you can know the world.
Without looking out the window,
    you can see heaven.

The farther you travel, the less you know.
Thus the wise person knows without traveling,
    understands without seeing,
        accomplishes without acting.

48

In the pursuit of learning,
    every day something is added.
In the pursuit of Tao,
    every day something is dropped.
Less and less is done, until
    one arrives at nonaction.
When nothing is done,
    nothing is left undone.

The world is won by letting things
    take their own course.
If you still have ambitions,
    it's out of your reach.

The sage has no set mind.
She adopts the concerns of others as her own.

She is good to the good.
She is also good to the bad.
This is real goodness.

She trusts the trustworthy.
She also trusts the untrustworthy.
This is real trust.

The sage takes the minds of the worldly
     and spins them around.
People drop their ideas and agendas,
     and she guides them like beloved children.

50

Between their births and their deaths,
      three out of ten are attached to life,
      three out of ten are attached to death,
      three out of ten are just idly passing through.
Only one knows how to die and stay dead
      and still go on living.

That one hasn't any ambitions,
      hasn't any ideas, makes no plans.
From this mysterious place of not-knowing
      and not-doing he gives birth to whatever
      is needed in the moment.
Because he is constantly filling his being
      with nonbeing, he can travel the wilds
      without worrying about tigers or wild
      buffalo, or he can cross a battlefield
      without armor or weapon.

No tiger can claw him.
No buffalo can gore him.
No weapon can pierce him.

Why is this so?
Because he has died, there isn't any more
room for death in him.

51

Tao gives life to all beings.
Nature nourishes them.
Fellow creatures shape them.
Circumstances complete them.

Everything in existence respects Tao
        and honors nature—
                not by decree, but spontaneously.

Tao gives life to all beings.
Nature watches over them,
        develops them,
                shelters them,
                        nurses them,
                                grows them,
                                        ripens them,
                                                completes them,
                                                        buries them,
                                                                and returns them.

Giving birth,
    nourishing life,
    shaping things without possessing them,
    serving without expectation of reward,
    leading without dominating:
These are the profound virtues of nature,
    and of nature's best beings.

52

The origin and mother of everything
    in the world is Tao.
Know the mother and you can know the children.
Having known the children, return to their
    source and hold on to her.
Abiding by the mother, you are free from
    danger, even when your body dies.

Don't live for your senses.
Close your mouth, close all the body's
    openings, and reside in the original unity.
In this way you can pass your whole life
    in peace and contentment.

Open your mouth, increase your activities,
    start making distinctions between things,
        and you'll toil forever without hope.

See the subtle and be illuminated.
Abide in gentleness and be strong.
Use your light, and return to insight.
Don't expose yourself to trouble.
This is following Tao.

53

Because I have a little wisdom,
    I choose to walk the great path of Tao
        and fear nothing except to stray from it.

The great way is very smooth and easy,
    but some people are fond of getting sidetracked.

When a ruler's palace is full of treasure,
    the people's fields are weedy and
        their granaries are empty.
If the ruler wears fancy clothes and
    his house is full of weapons,
        if his table is laden with extravagant
            food and drink and everywhere one
            looks he has more wealth than
            he can use, the ruler is a
            robber and a thief.
This is not in keeping with Tao.

54

Plant yourself firmly in the Tao and
    you won't ever be uprooted.
Embrace Tao firmly and you won't ever
    be separated from it.
Your children will thrive,
    and your children's children.

Cultivate goodness in your self,
    and goodness will be genuine.
Cultivate it in your family,
    and goodness will flourish.
Cultivate it in your community,
    and goodness will grow and multiply.
Cultivate it in your country,
    and goodness will be abundant.
Cultivate it in the world,
    and goodness will be everywhere.

How do I know the world works like this?
By watching.

She who is filled with goodness
    is like a newborn child:
        wasps and snakes will not bite it,
        fierce beasts will not attack it,
        birds of prey will not pounce on it.

Its bones are soft and its muscles weak,
    but its grip is firm.
It hasn't yet known the union of male and female,
    yet its organ stirs with vitality.
It can howl all day without becoming hoarse,
    so perfect is its harmony.

To know harmony is to know the eternal.
To know the eternal is to be illuminated.

Prolonging life is not harmonious.
Coercing the breath is unnatural.
Things which are overdeveloped must decay.
All this is contrary to Tao, and whatever
    is contrary to Tao soon ceases to be.

56

Those who know don't talk.
Those who talk don't know.

Close your mouth.
Block the door.
Quiet your senses.
Blunt the sharpness.
Untie the tangles.
Soften the brightness.
Be one with the dust,
    and enter the primal oneness.

One who has merged with Tao in this way
    can't be courted,
    can't be bought,
    can't be harmed,
    can't be honored,
    can't be humiliated.
He is the treasure of the world.

Govern a nation by following nature.
Fight a war with unexpected moves.
Win the world by letting go.

How do I know this? From seeing these:
The more prohibitions there are,
      the poorer people become.
The more weapons there are,
      the darker things become.
The more cunning and cleverness there is,
      the crazier things become.
The more laws there are,
      the greater the number of scoundrels.

Therefore the sage says:
I take no action,
      and people transform themselves.
I love tranquility,
      and people naturally do what is right.
I don't interfere,
      and people prosper on their own.
I have no desires,
      and people return to simplicity.

58

When the government is dull and sleepy,
     people are wholesome and good.
When the government is sharp and exacting,
     people are cunning and mean.

Good rests on bad.
Bad hides within good.
Who knows where the turning point is?

Whether government or person,
     if you aren't tranquil and honest,
     the normal flips to the abnormal,
     the auspicious reverts to the bizarre,
     and your bewilderment lasts for a long time.

Therefore the sage does what is right
     without acting righteous,
     points without piercing,
     straightens without straining,
     enlightens without dazzling.

In governing people and serving heaven,
    there is nothing better than moderation.

To be moderate is to follow Tao without straying.
To follow Tao without straying is to
    become filled with good energy.
To become filled with good energy is to
    overcome all things.
To overcome all things is to know that
    all things are possible.

She who knows that all things are possible
    is fit to govern people.
Because she is one with the mother,
    her roots go deep,
        her foundation stands firm,
        her life lasts long,
            her vision endures.

60

Governing a large country is like
    cooking a small fish.
If it's done in accordance with Tao,
    nothing bad will happen.

Guide the world with Tao,
    and evil won't be a problem.
Not that it won't be around,
    but it won't find an opening.
When it can't find an opening,
    it can't harm anyone.

The sage doesn't harm anyone, either.
When there's no harm on this side,
    no harm on that,
    goodness flows back and forth like water.

61

A great country is like low-lying land
    into which many streams flow.
It draws powerful energies to it as a
    receptive woman draws an eager man.

The feminine can always conquer the masculine
    by yielding and taking the lower position.
In this way she becomes as low-lying land:
    in time, everything comes her way.

Therefore a great country can win over a
    small country by practicing humility.
A small country can also win over a great
    country by practicing humility.
One wins by willingly taking the lower position.
The other wins by willingly acknowledging
    its lower position.

The great country wants to embrace and
    nourish more people.
The small country wants to ably serve
    its benefactor.

Both accomplish their ends by yielding.

62

Tao is the hidden secret source of all life.
Good men recognize that Tao provides for them
        and therefore they esteem it.
Bad men don't recognize this, but the Tao
        doesn't stop providing for them.

Beautiful words win some men honors;
        good deeds buy others acclaim.
But the Tao values everyone, not just
        those who excel.
What's the sense in discarding anyone?

Thus, on the day a new king is crowned
        or powerful ministers installed,
while others rush forward with gifts and praises,
        just be still and offer Tao.

Why have sages prized Tao for so long?
Because with Tao, he who seeks finds,
        and he who has flaws is forgiven.
This is why it is the treasure of the world.

63

Act by not acting,
  accomplish by not straining,
    understand by not knowing.
Regard the humble as exalted
  and the exalted as humble.
Remedy injury with tranquil repair.

Meet the difficult while it is still easy;
  cross the universe one step at a time.
Because the sage doesn't try anything too big,
  she's able to accomplish big things.

Those who commit lightly seldom come through.
Those who think everything is easy
  will find everything hard.
The sage understands that everything is difficult,
  and thus in the end has no difficulties.

64

What has equilibrium is easy to maintain.
What hasn't begun is easy to plan.
What is fragile is easy to shatter.
What is small is easy to scatter.

Deal with things before they arise.
Cultivate order before confusion sets in.

The greatest tree springs from a tiny shoot.
The tallest tower is built from a pile of dirt.
A journey of a thousand miles begins at your feet.

Interfere with things, and you'll be
        defeated by them.
Hold on to things, and you'll lose them.
The sage doesn't interfere, so he doesn't fail;
        doesn't hold on, so he doesn't lose.

Because projects often come to ruin
        just before completion,
he takes as much care at the end as
        he did at the beginning,
                and thereby succeeds.

His only desire is to be free of desire.
Fancying nothing,
        learning not to know,
                electing not to interfere,
                        he helps all beings become themselves.

65

In ancient times those who practiced Tao
       didn't want to enlighten people,
       but to keep them natural and simple.

When cleverness and intellect abound,
       people don't do well.
A leader who governs with cleverness
       cheats his people.
A leader who governs with simplicity
       is a blessing to his people.

These are the two alternatives.
Understanding them is subtle insight.
The use of subtle insight brings
       all things back into the oneness.

66

The sea is king of the valleys and streams
      because it is willing to be beneath them.
One who wishes to guide the people
      should be humble in her speech toward them.
One who wishes to lead the people
      must learn the art of following them.

The sage is above the people,
      but they don't feel her weight.
She stays ahead of the people,
      and no harm comes to them.
She has the affection of the whole world.
Because she contends with no one,
      no one can contend with her.

67

Everyone under heaven says that my Tao
      is great, but inconceivable.
It is its very greatness that makes
      it inconceivable!
If it could be conceived of,
      how small it would be!

I have three treasures to hold and protect:
The first is motherly love.
The second is economy.
The third is daring not to be first in the world.

With motherly love one can be courageous.
With economy one can be expansive.
With humility one can lead.

To be courageous without motherly love,
To be expansive without practicing economy,
To go to the front without humility—
      this is courting death.

Venture with love and you win the battle.
Defend with love and you are invulnerable.
Heaven's secret is motherly love.

68

A good general doesn't show off his power.
A good warrior doesn't get angry.
A good conqueror doesn't attack people.
A good employer puts himself below his
      employees.

This is called the power of noncontention.
This is called using the strength of others.
This is called perfect emulation of heaven.

In conflict it is better to be receptive
     than aggressive, better to retreat a foot
     than advance an inch.

This is called moving ahead without advancing,
     capturing the enemy without attacking him.

There is no greater misfortune than
     underestimating your opponent.
To underestimate your opponent is to
     forsake your three treasures.

When opposing forces are engaged in conflict,
     the one who fights with sorrow will triumph.

70

My words are very easy to understand,
  very easy to put into practice.
But you can't "understand" them,
  can't put them into "practice."

Words have their ruler.
Events have their origins.
People who can't understand this
  can't understand me.

The ones who do are few.
They wear coarse cloth and
  carry jade in their breasts.

Moving from knowing to not knowing—
    this is good.
Moving from not knowing to knowing—
    this is sickness.

You have to become sick of your sickness
    before you can get rid of it.

The sage isn't sick.
He's sick of his sickness.
Therefore he's not sick.

72

If people fear your power,
      then you don't really have any.

Leave them alone in their homes.
Respect them in their lives,
      and they won't grow weary of you.

The sage knows herself,
      but doesn't dwell on herself;
Loves herself, but no more than
      she loves everyone else.

She adopts the concerns of heaven
      as her own.

73

Those who are courageous out of daring
    are killed.
Those who are courageous out of love
    survive.
The first is harmful, the second beneficial.

Heaven prohibits some things,
    but who knows the reason?
Not even the sage knows the answer to this.

This is the way of heaven:
It doesn't contend, but easily overcomes.
It doesn't speak, but always responds.
It can't be summoned, but comes of
    its own volition.
Utterly without haste, it plans for everything.

The net of heaven is vast.
Though its meshes are wide,
    nothing slips through.

74

If people don't love life,
      they won't fear death,
      and threatening them with it won't work.

If people have lives worth living,
      then the threat of death is meaningful,
      and they'll do what is right to avoid it.

But killing itself should be the province of the
      great executioner alone.
Trying to take his place and kill
      is like cutting wood in the place
      of the master carpenter:
The odds are you'll hurt your own hand.

75

What makes people go hungry?
Rulers eating up all the money in taxes.

What makes people rebellious?
Rulers who can't stop interfering.

What makes people take death so lightly?
People taking life so seriously.

Those who enjoy life are wiser than
    those who employ life.

76

At birth a person is soft and yielding,
    at death stiff and hard.
All beings, the grass, the trees:
    alive, soft, and yielding;
    dead, stiff, and hard.

Therefore the hard and inflexible
    are friends of death.
The soft and yielding
    are friends of life.

An unyielding army is destroyed.
An unbending tree breaks.

The hard must humble itself
    or be otherwise humbled.
The soft will ultimately ascend.

77

The way of heaven is like the bending
     of a bow.
What is high up gets pulled down.
What is low down gets pulled up.

Heaven takes from what has too much and
     gives to what doesn't have enough.
Man is different:
     he takes from those who have too little
     and gives to those who have too much.

Who has a genuine abundance to give to the world?
Only a person of Tao.

He acts without expectation,
     accomplishes without taking credit,
     and has no desire to display his merit.

78

Nothing under heaven is as
    soft and yielding as water.
Yet for attacking the hard and strong,
    nothing can compare with it.

The weak overcomes the strong.
The soft overcomes the hard.
Everyone knows this, but none
    have the ability to practice it.

Therefore the sage says:
One who accepts the dung of the nation
    becomes the master of soil and sustenance.
One who deals with the evils of the nation
    becomes king under heaven.

True words seem paradoxical.

In the reconciling of resentments,
   ill will often lingers.
What's the good in that?

The person who is truly good concerns
   herself always with what she owes others,
   never with what they owe her.

The Tao of heaven is impartial.
If you perpetuate it, it perpetuates you.

80

Let there be small countries with few people.
Let the people have no use for complicated
    machinery.
Let them be mindful of death so that they
      don't move too far from their birthplaces.
If there are boats and carriages,
      let there be nowhere to take them to.
If there are weapons,
      let there be no occasion to display them.
Let the people's responsibilities be few
      enough that they may remember them
      by knotting a string.
Let them enjoy their food,
      be content with their clothes,
         be satisfied with their homes,
            and take pleasure in their customs.
Though the next country may be close enough
      to hear the barking of its dogs and the
         crowing of its rooster, let the people
            grow old and die without feeling compelled
               to visit it.

True words aren't elaborate.
Elaborate words aren't true.

Good people don't argue.
People who argue aren't good.

People who know aren't full of facts.
People who are full of facts don't know.

The sage doesn't hoard.
She increases her treasure by
    working for her fellow human beings.
She increases her abundance by
    giving herself to them.

The way of heaven:
    benefit all, harm none.
The way of the sage:
    work for all, contend with none.